Contents

How to use this book

Each page has a title telling you what it is about.

Instructions look like this. Always read these carefully before starting.

Read these word problems very carefully. Decide how you will work out the answers.

This shows you how to set out your work. The first question is done for you.

This is Owl. Ask your teacher if you need to do his questions.

These are exploratory activities. You may want to discuss them with a partner.

Sequences

Write the missing numbers.

1. | 4 4 . . .

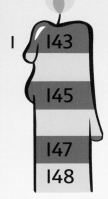
1
143
145
147
148

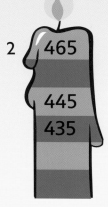
2
465
542
445
435

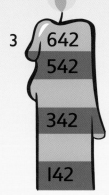
3
642
542
342
142

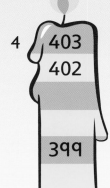
4
403
402
399

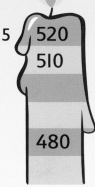
5
520
510
480

Write the next four numbers in each sequence.

6. 370, 380, 390, 400

6 340 350 360

7 9678 8678 7678

8 3241 3242 3243

9 4307 4207 4107

10 763 773 783

11 8642 8632 8622

12 1586 1587 1588

13 663 763 863

Write five different sequences,
each containing the number 3967.

3

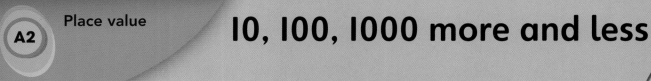

10, 100, 1000 more and less

The crosses are part of a number square. Write the missing numbers.

1. 119, 128

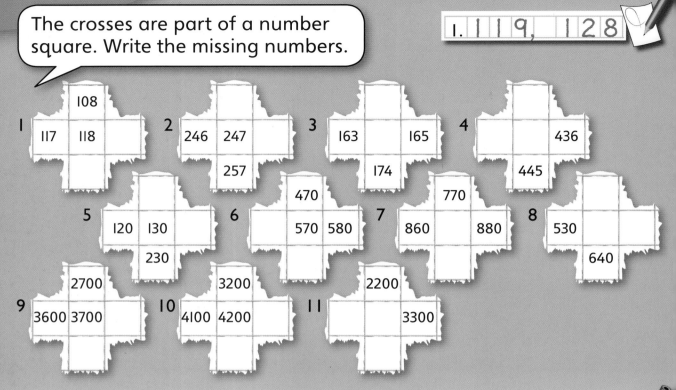

1
	108	
117	118	

2
246	247	
	257	

3
163		165
	174	

4
		436
	445	

5
120	130	
	230	

6
	470	
570	580	

7
	770	
860		880

8
530		
		640

9
2700	
3600	3700

10
3200	
4100	4200

11
2200	
	3300

Complete each step.

12. 4748, 4648, 5648

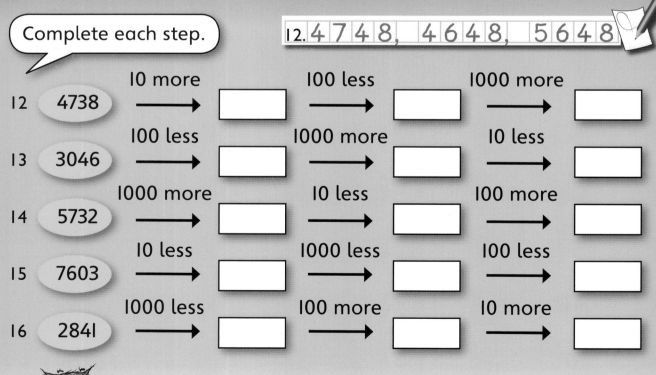

#	start			
12	4738	→10 more	→100 less	→1000 more
13	3046	→100 less	→1000 more	→10 less
14	5732	→1000 more	→10 less	→100 more
15	7603	→10 less	→1000 less	→100 less
16	2841	→1000 less	→100 more	→10 more

Invent some steps so that you finish on the number 3582.

Adding and subtracting 10, 100, 1000

A2

Look at each number. Roll a dice. Add or subtract to match the dice throw.

1. 4732 + 100 = 4832

 add 10

 subtract 100

 add 1000

 add 100

 subtract 1000

 subtract 10

1 4732
2 4461
3 3890
4 4690
5 5943
6 1207
7 8054
8 7321
9 6666

Which of these numbers becomes 5000 after adding 10, 100 and 1000?

Explore

Use a set of cards: 0 1 2 3 4 5 6 7 8 9

and an extra 2 and 3.

Create two 4-digit numbers that have a difference of 10.

One number must use the 0 card.

How many can you make? 2 5 9 3   2 6 0 3

Repeat for numbers that have a difference of 100, and of 1000.

5

Adding and subtracting 10, 100, 1000

Write the new mileage after these journeys.

`1.4832`

1 `4732` 100 miles

2 `8683` 10 miles

3 `5742` 1000 miles

4 `4796` 10 miles

5 `3807` 1000 miles

6 `1973` 100 miles

7 `17085` 1000 miles

8 `46835` 100 miles

9 `21691` 10 miles

10 Write a mileage so that after 10 more miles, three digits have to change.

What year is:

11 10 years earlier than **1993**

12 100 years later than **1996**

13 1000 years before **2006**

14 a decade later than **1066**

15 a century earlier than **1873**

16 a millennium after **1765**

17 Write the date 10 years from today.

18 Write the date 10 years ago. Repeat for 100 years and 1000 years.

Invent some date questions to ask your partner. Write one down with an answer.

Ordering

Write < or > between each pair of train numbers.

1. 4 7 3 < 5 2 1

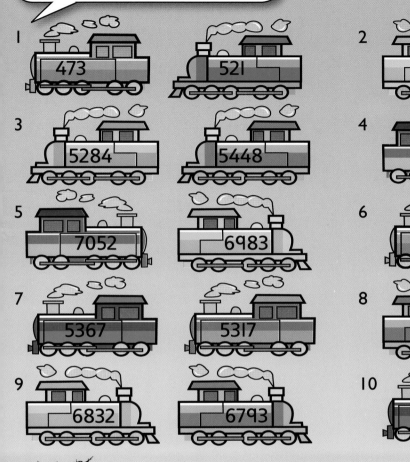

1   473   521

2   357   385

3   5284   5448

4   9376   9295

5   7052   6983

6   4006   3997

7   5367   5317

8   4603   4652

9   6832   6793

10 9413   9409

Write any number that lies between each pair.

Write all the numbers between:

11. 7 1 3, 7 1 4, 7 1 5

11 712 and 716

12 896 and 903

13 529 and 534

14 997 and 1005

15 3828 and 3834

16 3297 and 3302

Ordering

Match the numbers to the pointers on the line. Write the letter beside the number.

1. 7735 : v

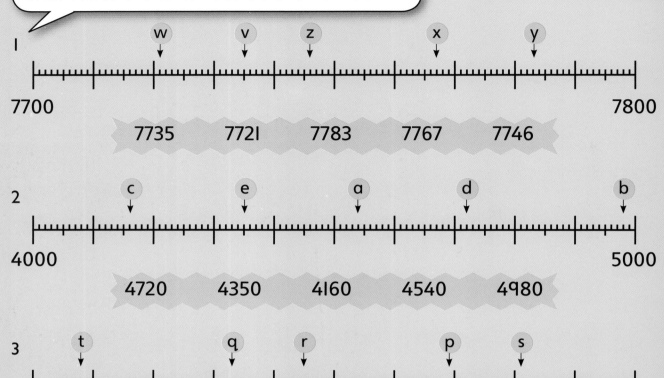

1
```
w          v          z              x          y
```
7700 ←——————————————————————————————————————→ 7800

7735   7721   7783   7767   7746

2
```
c          e          a          d          b
```
4000 ←——————————————————————————————————————→ 5000

4720   4350   4160   4540   4980

3
```
t              q      r          p      s
```
56 300 ←——————————————————————————————————————→ 56 400

56 381   56 345   56 308   56 369   56 333

Explore

Use number cards: 3 7 2 5

How many numbers can you create between 4000 and 8000?

Write them in order.

Now use cards: 5 4 6 1 9

Try to make 20 numbers between 55 000 and 65 000.

Ordering

For each set of amounts, write (a) the smallest and (b) the largest.

1. (a) £2716 (b) £6093

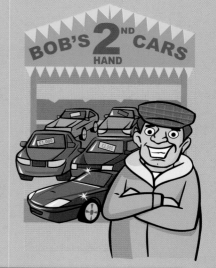

1	£5261	£4372	£2716	£3847	£6093
2	£8242	£8457	£8912	£8046	£8535
3	£2608	£2675	£2632	£2659	£2593
4	£4706	£4710	£4709	£4703	£4712
5	£35276	£33482	£34179	£33946	£34082
6	£70100	£70001	£71000	£70101	£70010

Pick 10 amounts. Write them in order, smallest to largest.

Explore

Use these cards to make a number:

7 3 2 6

7 more than 7500

2 8 1 4

8 less than 1500

2 8 6 4 3

9 more than 31000

7 5 3 9 8

10 less than 48000

6 3 8 5 4

11 between 45300 and 45400

7 2 3 6 1

12 between 17500 and 18000

For each set of cards make a number as near to 6000 as you can. You do not have to use all of the cards each time.

Ordering

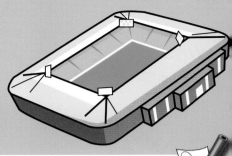

1 These are the numbers of spectators at each team's first five matches.
Write them in order, smallest to largest.

1. Portsmath: 2 9 5 7 6, ...

	Portsmath	Real Mathid	Math United
match 1	32 567	86 540	72 564
match 2	30 482	83 460	71 936
match 3	33 291	79 280	74 285
match 4	29 576	83 540	72 049
match 5	33 910	83 490	74 036

For match 1, write how many more are needed to make each number a round 'hundred' or 'thousand'.

Write the number that is exactly half-way between each pair.

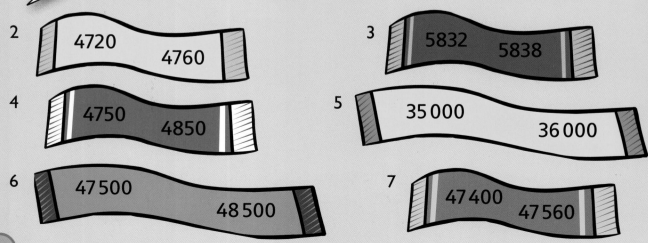

2 4720   4760

3 5832   5838

4 4750   4850

5 35 000   36 000

6 47 500   48 500

7 47 400   47 560

Odd or even?

Write 'odd' or 'even' for each number.

1. odd

1. 43
2. 76
3. 257
4. 384
5. 90
6. 168
7. 1599
8. 3740
9. 28531
10. 47325
11. 65000
12. 73999

Write the next two odd numbers each time.

13. 49, 51

13. 47
14. 931
15. 259
16. 4163
17. 2865
18. 7323
19. 41525
20. 28369

Write the next two even numbers each time.

21. 56
22. 738
23. 450
24. 294
25. 696
26. 2610
27. 43152
28. 21498

Use a set of 0–9 number cards. Make five different 2-digit even numbers, so that when you put them in order they differ from each other by 22.

Odd or even?

1 For each circled yellow number, find three different pairs of:

1. (a) $26 = 14 + 12...$

a **yellow numbers with that total**

b **blue numbers with that total.**

c **Try to find one yellow and one blue number with that total.**

1	2	3	4	5	6	7	8	9	10
11	12	13	14	15	16	17	18	19	20
21	22	23	24	25	(26)	27	28	29	30
31	32	33	34	35	36	37	38	39	40
41	42	43	44	(45)	46	47	48	49	50
51	(52)	53	54	55	56	57	58	59	60
61	62	63	64	65	66	67	68	69	70
71	72	73	74	75	76	77	(78)	79	80
81	82	(83)	84	85	86	87	88	89	90
91	92	93	94	95	96	97	98	99	100

2 Repeat for each circled blue number.

Write 'odd' or 'even' for each answer.

3. odd

3 68 + 75

4 931 + 428

5 359 − 176

6 8453 − 2172

7 1362 + 2519

8 4738 − 3542

9 684 732 − 153 286

10 7436 + 2879 + 1345

11 5 867 293 − 73 584

12 486 732 − 1458

Write the units digit for each answer.

Write three different calculations with an odd answer, and three with an even answer.

Odd or even?

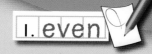

Write 'odd' or 'even' for each answer.

1 odd + odd =

2 even + even =

3 even + odd =

4 odd + even =

5 even − even =

6 even − odd =

7 odd − even =

8 odd − odd =

9 odd + odd + odd =

10 even + even + even =

11 even + odd + even =

12 odd + even + odd =

Write some sentences like this for adding four numbers.

Write 'odd' or 'even' for each hidden card.

Each set has an odd total.

13  7

14  13

15  9

16  15 16

17  3 13

18 45 62

Each set has an even total.

19  8

20  11

21  27

22  15 19

23  63 28

24  42 19

Odd or even?

3 and 5, 11 and 13 are consecutive
(next-door) odd numbers.
2 and 4, 16 and 18 are consecutive even numbers.

1. 5 and 7

Find two consecutive odd numbers with these totals:

1 12   2 28   3 16   4 40   5 20   6 48

Find two consecutive even numbers with these totals:

7 10   8 18   9 30   10 38   11 62   12 50

Find some totals of three consecutive numbers.
What patterns do you notice in the totals?

We are number cards 0 to 9. Guess who we are.

13 We are both even. Our total is 14.

14 We are both odd. Our difference is
    4 and our total is less than 12.

15 One of us is odd and one even. Our total is 11
    and our difference is 1.

16 We are both odd. Our difference is 6.
    One of us is 3 times the other.

17 We are all odd. Our total is 15. One of
    us is half the total of the other two.

Invent some clues of your own.

Positive and negative numbers

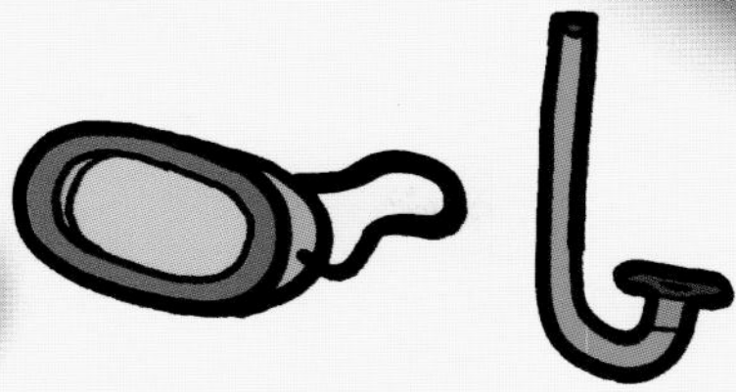

Write the position of each flag.

1. (a) 3

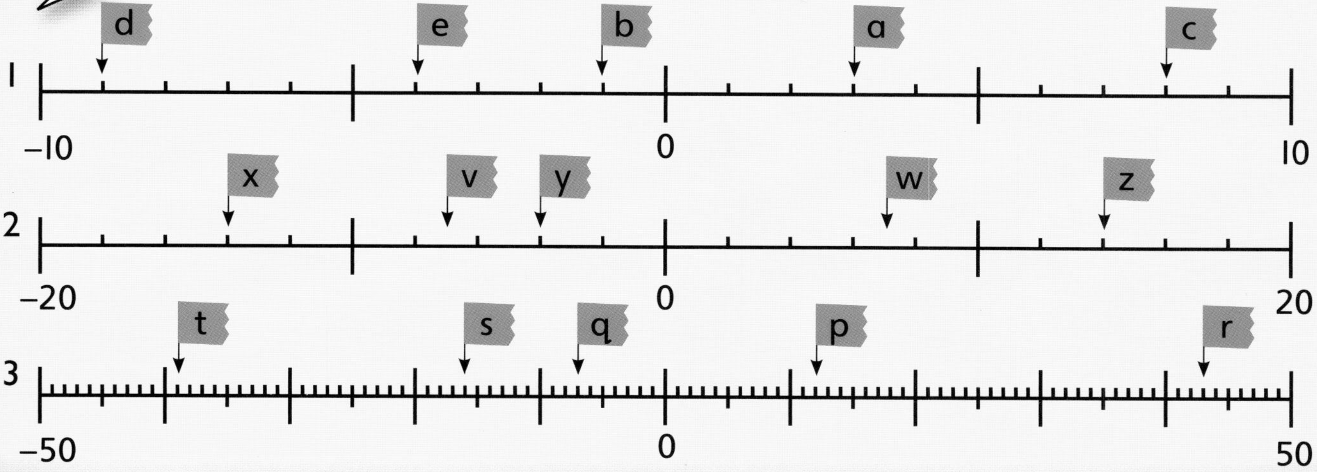

1 | d ↓   e ↓   b ↓   a ↓   c ↓

−10   0   10

2 | x ↓   v ↓   y ↓   w ↓   z ↓

−20   0   20

3 | t ↓   s ↓   q ↓   p ↓   r ↓

−50   0   50

Write the next four numbers in each sequence.

4. 0, −1, −2, −3

4.  2, 1

5. −3, −4, −5

6. −10, −9, −8

7. 20, 15, 10

8. −10, −8, −6

9. 16, 12, 8

10. 3, 1, −1

Write three of your own sequences that have positive and negative numbers.

Positive and negative numbers

Write the temperature each animal lives at.

1

| °C | 40° |
| 30° |
| 20° |
| 10° |
| 0° |
| –10° |

2

| °C | 40° |
| 30° |
| 20° |
| 10° |
| 0° |
| –10° |

3

| °C | 40° |
| 30° |
| 20° |
| 10° |
| 0° |
| –10° |

4

| °C | 30° |
| 20° |
| 10° |
| 0° |
| –10° |
| –20° |

5

| °C | 30° |
| 20° |
| 10° |
| 0° |
| –10° |
| –20° |

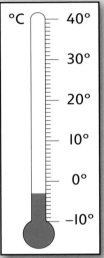
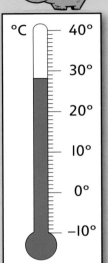
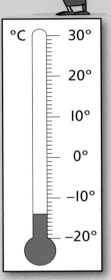
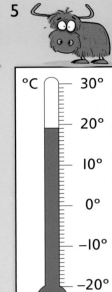

Write these in order, smallest to largest.

6. –10, –5, ...

6
4   –5
   7   –3
–10   –1

7
      0
–2   8   3
   –6   –11

8
      –73
85   58
   –37
–58   37

9
      7°C
–4°C   –11°C
      0°C
3°C

10
28°C   7°C   –1°C
   –9°C   1°C

11
64   0
      –2
   5   –64

12   Write the difference between the smallest and largest each time.

 Write five different pairs of positive and negative numbers that have a difference of 6.

Positive and negative numbers

This shows the temperature at different places on the same day.

Write the temperature in:

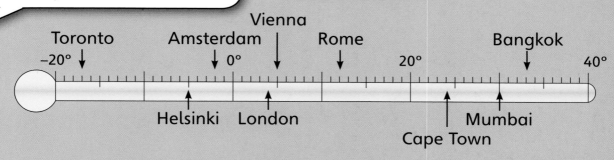

1 Vienna

2 Helsinki

3 Mumbai

4 Toronto

5 Cape Town

6 Amsterdam

Write how much warmer or colder it is in:

7 Vienna than London

8 Rome than Toronto

9 Mumbai than Amsterdam

10 Helsinki than Cape Town

11 Toronto than Bangkok

12 Amsterdam than Helsinki

Write the difference between:

13 7°C and 11°C

14 −3°C and 5°C

15 −6°C and −10°C

16 0°C and −5°C

17 −13°C and 13°C

18 −5°C and 9°C

Work with a partner. Discuss what today's temperature might be. How cold does it get in winter? How hot does it get in summer? What is the difference?

Positive and negative numbers

Write the new temperature.

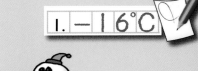
1. – 1 6 °C

1
−21°C
rises 5°

2
2°C
falls 9°

3
−3°C
rises 7°

4
38°C
rises 6°

5
−12°C
rises 7°

6
−4°C
falls 9°

7
24°C
falls 11°
then rises 4°

8
−7°C
rises 9°
then falls 4°

9
−11°C
falls 4°
then rises 7°

Write five different ways of finishing with a temperature of 2°C.

10 Su went to bed and the temperature fell by 15°C overnight. At lunchtime it had risen by 6°C, to 18°C. What was the temperature when Su went to bed?

11 It was 21°C at home, but then there was a power cut. The temperature dropped 3° every 30 minutes. What was the temperature of the room after 3 hours?

12 Adam took the peas out of the freezer, where the temperature was −18°C. The temperature of the peas rose by 2° every 20 minutes. How long did they take to reach 0°C?

Doubling and halving

Write these numbers after they come out of the doubling machine.

1.6 ✓

1	3	2	7
3	5	4	8
5	4	6	9
7	2	8	6

9	30	10	40	11	15	12	45
13	35	14	50	15	70	16	25

Put some fractions through the machine, for example $\frac{1}{2}$, $\frac{1}{4}$, $\frac{2}{3}$.

Write these numbers before they went into the machine.

17.3 ✓

17	6	18	10	19	16	20	12
21	14	22	18	23	40	24	50
25	80	26	70	27	30	28	90

Which number does not change when it goes through the machine?

Doubling and halving

Double these numbers by doubling the tens, doubling the units, then combining.

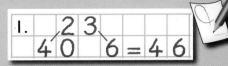

1. 2 3
    4 0   6 = 4 6

1 23	2 31	3 44	4 12
5 16	6 27	7 38	8 19
9 28	10 36	11 49	12 57

Halve these numbers by halving the tens, halving the units, then combining.

13. 4 8
     2 0   4 = 2 4

13 48	14 26	15 46	16 82
17 34	18 58	19 76	20 38
21 92	22 64	23 72	24 54

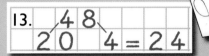

Write the cost of two of each item.

25. 2 × £ 3 2 = £ 6 4

25 £32   26   27 £48   28 £38   29 £18 £2...

Write the cost of each item in a half-price sale.

Find the cost of five of each item by halving the cost of ten of each. How could you find the cost of 20 of one of the items?

Near doubles

Use doubling to complete these additions.

1. double 34 = 68
      35 + 34 = 69

1 double 34 =
   34 + 35 =

2 double 42 =
   42 + 41 =

3 double 26 =
   26 + 27 =

4 double 18 =
   18 + 19 =

5 double 23 =
   23 + 22 =

6 double 45 =
   45 + 44 =

7 double 28
   28 + 27 =

8 double 37 =
   37 + 36 =

9 double 46 =
   46 + 47 =

Write a near double for each of these numbers.

10. double 31 + 1

10 63

11 31

12 45

13 29

14 87

15 53

16 71

17 95

Guess who I am:

18 I am a number less than 20. When I am doubled the answer is 6 multiplied by itself.

19 I am a number greater than 40. When I am halved the answer is double 12.

20 I am a number less than 15. When I am doubled the answer is the seventh multiple of 4.

21 I am a number greater than 50. When I am halved the answer is the number of days in March.

Invent some 'Guess who I am' problems.

Doubles and halves

The outer ring on these dartboards counts double. Write the scores on each.

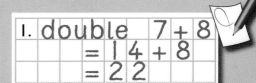

1. double 7 + 8
   = 14 + 8
   = 22

1 4 7
   8
5
6 9

2 4 7
      8
5
6 9

3 16 13
   15   12
   14 11

4 26 21
   25 22
   24 23

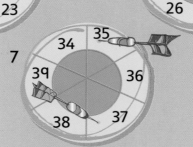

5 28 23
   27 24
   26 25

6 36 31
   35 32
   34 33

7 35
   34 36
   39
   38 37

8 43 42
   44 41
   45 46

Write the scores on each board if the inner ring counts treble.

Explore

Use number cards: 1 2 3 4 5 6 7 8

Make pairs of 2-digit numbers so that one is double the other.

How many pairs can you find? 3 1   6 2

How many more can you find by including 0 and 9 ?

Doubles and halves

> Double both cards. Put them together to make a double.

1. 360
   600 120 = 720

1 3 0 0 6 0

2 1 0 0 8 0

3 4 0 2 0 0

4 2 0 4 0 0

5 2 0 0 6 0

6 7 0 3 0 0

7 1 0 0 6 0

8 4 0 3 0 0

9 2 0 0 9 0

> Double each number by writing it as a number of tens.

10. 43 tens → 86 tens → 860

10 430

11 340

12 220

13 320

14 450

15 240

16 410

17 330

18 280

19 390

20 470

21 360

Start with 20 and keep doubling. How far can you go? Try starting with 30.

Doubles and halves

These are the distances between two places. Write the distance for each return journey.

1.
```
   440
800   80
=880 miles
```

1
Edinburgh to Exeter
440 miles

2
Newcastle to Southampton
320 miles

3
Harwich to Dover
130 miles

4
Glasgow to Lincoln
270 miles

5
Aberdeen to Hull
360 miles

6
Penzance to Shrewsbury
280 miles

7
Nottingham to Southampton
160 miles

8
Liverpool to Oxford
170 miles

If £1 of petrol fuels a car for 5 miles, find the cost of two of these journeys.

How far apart are these places if this is the distance of a return journey?

9.
```
   480
200   40=240km
```

9   480 km

10   280 km

11   520 km

12   760 km

13   380 km

14   940 km

Which of these return journeys are longer than 300 miles?

Doubles and halves

Find the new price by halving the thousands and the hundreds separately.

1  £6800

2  £7400

3  £3600

4  £5200

5  £6100

6  £8600

7  £9400

8  £7800

If each price has £2500 taken off, for which cars would this be a better deal than paying half price?

Biggest fish Pie in the World

<u>Ingredients</u>
2800 mackerel
3400 crabs
4600 prawns
3800 potatoes
1400 l white sauce
4200 g pastry

To make a pie twice as big, write how much of these you will need:

9 crabs

10 potatoes

11 white sauce

12 pastry

13 prawns

14 mackerel

Write how much of each ingredient you need for a pie half as big.

Doubles and halves

> If the answer is correct, double your money.
> If it is incorrect, halve your money.

1.
£6800

How many sides has an octagon? 6

2.
£3600

What is the third multiple of 8? 24

3.
£2400

What is a quarter of a metre in centimetres? 25

4.
£7400

What is 48 divided by 6? 7

5.
£5600

How many seconds in three minutes? 160

6.
£1200

How many millilitres in $\frac{3}{4}$ of a litre? 750

7.
£4300

How many faces does a tetrahedron have? 4

8.
£1700

What must be added to 38 to make 100? 62

 Explore

To double the total:
either add them, then double the total
or double each, then add.

340 130

Check to see if both methods give the same answer.
Try it on your own pair of numbers.

Try both methods for halving a total.

Symmetry

Are these symmetrical patterns – yes or no?

1. Yes

1

2

3

4

5

6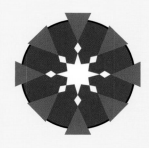

Copy the picture. Draw the other half to create a symmetrical pattern.

7.

7

8

9

10

11

12

Find something symmetrical in the room. Sketch half of it.

Symmetry

Copy each shape. Draw one line of symmetry on each.

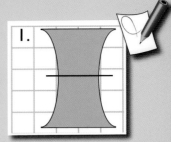

I.

1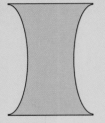

2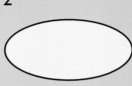

3

4

5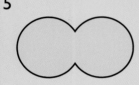

6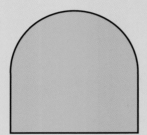

7

8

On which shapes can you draw two lines of symmetry?

 Explore

Draw a line of symmetry.

Draw a triangle on either side.

Build up a symmetrical pattern.

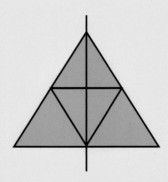

Symmetry

This is Bill's homework. Say which lines of symmetry he got wrong.

1
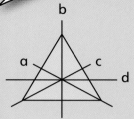

2
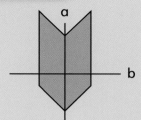

3
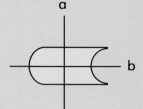

4
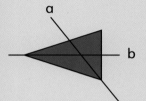

5
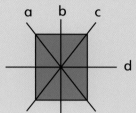

6
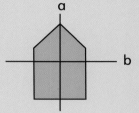

7
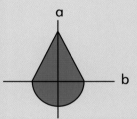

8
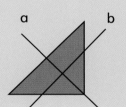

9
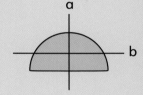

Copy each shape. Draw the reflection in the mirror line.

10
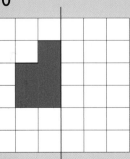

11
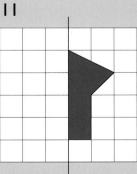

12
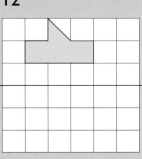

13
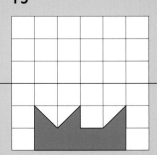

Draw an octagon with two lines of symmetry and two right angles.

29

Symmetry

1 Draw a quadrilateral with two lines of symmetry.

2 Draw a pentagon with one line of symmetry.

3 Draw a hexagon with two lines of symmetry.

4 Draw a kite with one line of symmetry.

5 Draw round a regular pentagon and draw in the lines of symmetry.

6 Draw a polygon with four lines of symmetry.

7 Draw a polygon with no lines of symmetry.

3D shapes

1 Match the names to the shapes.

1. (a) prism

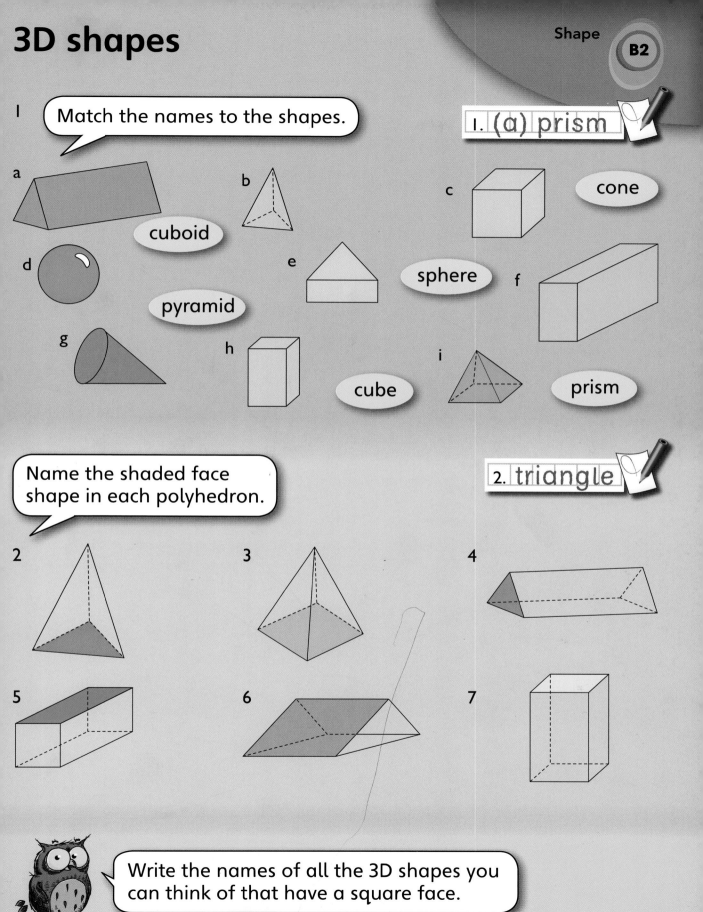

a

cuboid

b

c

cone

d

e

sphere

f

pyramid

g

h

i

cube

prism

Name the shaded face shape in each polyhedron.

2. triangle

2

3

4

5

6

7

Write the names of all the 3D shapes you can think of that have a square face.

3D shapes

1

Identify and name all the shapes in this sculpture.

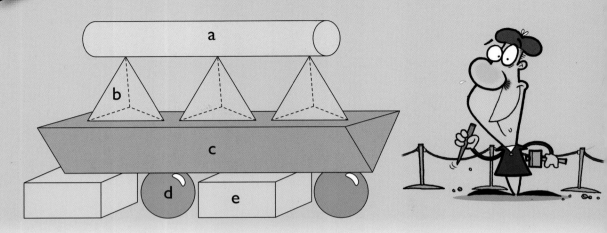

Work with a partner. Describe a 3D shape for them to identify. Take turns to describe and identify shapes.

2

Which shapes have:
- a triangular face
- a square face
- a rectangular face

2. triangular face: a, b, ...

a

b

c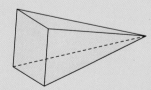

d

e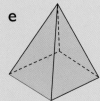

f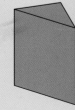

Write the total number of faces on each shape.

3D shapes

For each shape:

1 Name the shape.

2 Write the number of vertices.

3 Write the number of edges.

4 Write the number of faces.

Shape (a)
1. prism
2. 6 vertices ...

a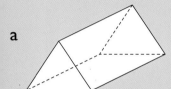

b

c

d

e

f

g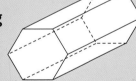

h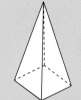

i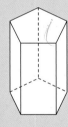

j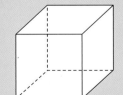

k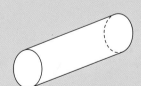

l

5 Which of these shapes have more faces than edges?

 With a partner, find examples of 3D shapes around the classroom. List the objects and write the shape name, for example: lampshade – cylinder.

3D shapes

Write the name of the shape made by each net.

1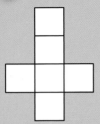

2

3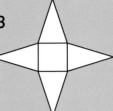

4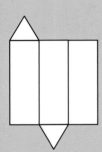

5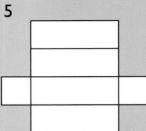

6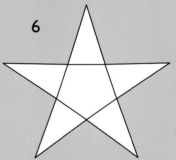

Explore

Which of these nets cannot be folded to make a cube?

7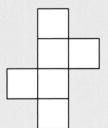

8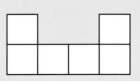

9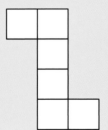

10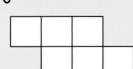

11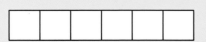

Check by copying them onto squared paper, cutting them out and folding.

Capacity

1
> List the containers that hold less than
> 1 litre and write how much they contain.

`1.(a)250 ml...`

a
250 ml

b
1200 ml

c
1500 ml

d
500 ml

e
100 ml

f
1 l

g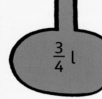
$\frac{3}{4}$ l

h
600 ml

> List the containers that hold less than half a litre.

> How many mugs (containing 250 ml)
> can be filled from a 2-pint bottle?

> In each pair, identify the container that holds more.

2

450 ml $\frac{1}{2}$ l

3

$\frac{1}{4}$ l   200 ml

4

1 l   600 ml

5

$\frac{3}{4}$ l   700 ml

6

850 ml   1 l

7

$\frac{1}{2}$ l   550 ml

Capacity

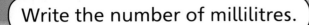 Write the number of millilitres.

1  $\frac{1}{2}$ l

2  $1\frac{1}{4}$ l

3  $\frac{1}{4}$ l

4  $\frac{3}{4}$ l

5  $1\frac{1}{2}$ l

6  $1\frac{3}{4}$ l

7  1 l

8  2 l

 How many cups of 100 ml can be filled from a 5 l bucket? What about from a 10 l bucket?

9 Match containers with the same amount.

9. a and h

a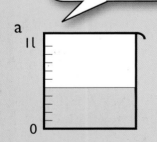

b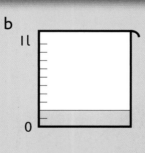

c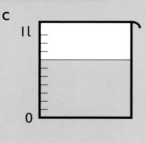

d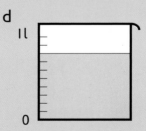

e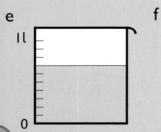

f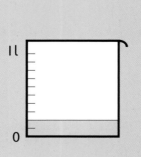

g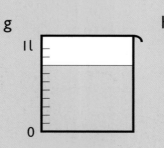

h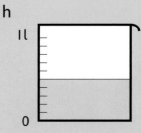

Capacity

1. A bottle contains 200 ml of shampoo. Beth uses 5 ml for each hair wash. How long will the bottle last if she washes her hair every day? How much longer would it last if she used 4 ml each day?

2. Dad fills a 100 l paddling pool with water. How many 1500 ml jugs will he need?

3. Amit uses 1500 ml of water to wash his dog. He does this once a week. How many litres does he use in 1 year?

4. How many 5 ml medicine spoonfuls can you get from a $1\frac{1}{4}$ l bottle of cough mixture?

If it takes 10 seconds for 1 l of water to run into a bath, how long does it take to fill a 160 l bath?

5. Match containers with the same amount.

5. a and e

a
300 ml

b
1 l 200 ml

c
500 ml

d
850 ml

e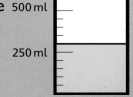
500 ml
250 ml

f
1 l
500 ml

g
1 l
500 ml

Timetables

Look at the timetable. Answer the children's questions.

Birmingham	Crewe	Pwllheli
9:30 am	11:35 am	4:50 pm
10:47 am	12:05 pm	6:10 pm
11:25 am	1:30 pm	6:55 pm

1 Which is the quickest train to Crewe from Birmingham?
2 What time do I leave Birmingham to get to Pwllheli before 5 o'clock?
3 Which train is fastest from Crewe to Pwllheli?
4 What is the latest I can leave Birmingham to be in Crewe before 1 o'clock?
5 How long will it take to get from Crewe to Pwllheli if I take the 1:30 pm train?
6 How long will it take to get from Birmingham to Pwllheli on the 10:47 train?

If each train is 10 minutes late, what are the new times?

7

It is the first day of Ian's life as an evacuee.

7. Getting up: 20 minutes

Work out and list how long each event lasts.

Work with a partner to write a timetable for your average school morning.

7:15	get up
7:35	breakfast
7:55	clean teeth
8:00	leave house
8:15	meet outside church hall
9:00	tour of village
9:50	visit school
10:30	tea in church rooms
12:00	go home

Timetables

Look at the timetable. Answer the questions.

	Monday	Tuesday	Wednesday	Thursday	Friday
9:00	English	Maths	English	Maths	English
10:45					
11:10	Maths	History/Geography	Maths	Science	CDT
12:20					
1:30	Art	English	R E	English	PE / Music
3:00					

1 What time is Science?

2 On which days do we have Maths?

3 How many times in the week do we have English?

Which lessons start at 1:30?

5 Which lessons last $1\frac{3}{4}$ hours?

6 Which are the longest lessons in the day? And the shortest?

7 How long do we spend doing English each week?

Work with a partner to write your own lesson timetable for the week.

3:00 go bowling
5:10 travel to cafe
5:20 start meal
6:45 travel to cinema
7:05 film starts
8:50 film ends

8   How long do we spend bowling?
9   Which part of the day takes longest?
10 How long do we spend travelling?
11 Which takes longer, the meal or the film?

Timetables

Look at these facts. Draw up a timetable.

1

HYPERSPACE TOURS

Rocket leaves
Moon
7:15 am
9:00 am
3:00 pm
6:00 pm

Rocket arrives
at Mars
11:00 am
12:20 pm
7:00 pm
12:00 midnight

Rocket arrives
at Jupiter
1:00 pm
3:40 pm
10:00 pm
7:25 am

2 Which is the quickest rocket to Mars?

3 What time do I reach Mars if I leave the Moon at 3:00 pm?

4 What is the latest time I can leave Mars to get to Jupiter?

5 What is the slowest rocket to Jupiter?

6 **Look at this timetable. Choose four journeys. Write how long each journey takes.**

LONDON ▶ ALL DESTINATIONS					Monday to Saturday		
Notes	London	Ashford	Calais	Lille	Brussels	Paris	Train
1	05.34	06.27				09.23	9078
1	06.10	06.59		08.56	09.37		9106
2	06.27	07.20		09.18	10.01		9108
	06.34	07.24	08.56			10.23	9002
1	07.09	07.59		09.56		10.59	9004

Timetables

1 Copy the timetable and fill in the gaps.

Tour timetable

Entrance	Zebras	Monkeys	Lions	Penguins
9:30	9:40	9:50	10:00	10:10
10:20	10:30			
12:15		12:35		
2:45			3:15	
4:05	4:15			

2 Draw up a timetable for the wardens.

We feed the tigers for an hour at 7:00 am and at 3:00 pm.

We clean out the tigers after we have fed them.

We give the baby tiger its vitamins at 10:00 am and at 5:00 pm.

It takes an hour to clean out the tigers.

It takes half an hour to provide fresh straw.

We provide fresh straw at 1:00 pm.

We shut the tigers in their house at 6:00 pm.

Perimeter

For each rectangle, write (a) the perimeter and (b) the area.

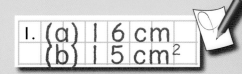

1. (a) 16 cm
   (b) 15 cm²

1
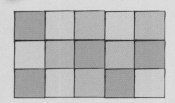

2
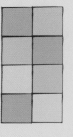

3
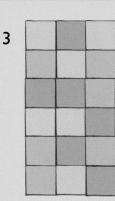

5
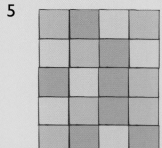

4
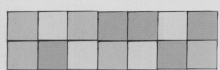

6
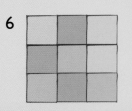

These carpet tiles have sides of length 1 m. Write the perimeter of each set of tiles.

7. 10 m

7

8

9

10
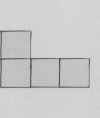

11

12
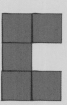

13
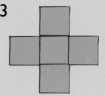

14
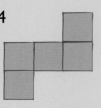

Draw some different arrangements of tiles that have a perimeter of 14 m.

Perimeter

 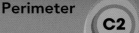

Write the perimeter of each name plate.

 1. 4 8 cm

1

12 cm
12 cm   12 cm
12 cm

2
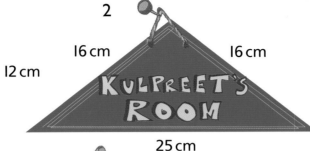
16 cm   16 cm
25 cm

3
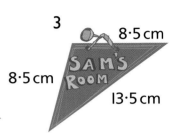
8·5 cm
8·5 cm
13·5 cm

4
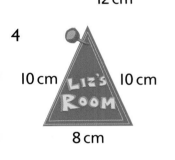
10 cm   10 cm
8 cm

5

9 cm   9 cm
9 cm
9 cm
9 cm

6

8 cm   8 cm
8 cm
8 cm   8 cm
8 cm

7

18 cm
8 cm   8 cm
18 cm

Write the perimeter of these rectangles:

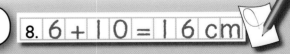 8. 6 + 10 = 16 cm

8   3 cm by 5 cm

9   4 cm by 2 cm

10 6 cm by 5 cm

11 7 cm by 10 cm

12 8 cm by 3 m

13 5 cm by 7 cm

14 4 cm by 2·5 cm

15 6·5 cm by 3·5 cm

16 2·5 cm by 9·5 cm

 Does half a 4 × 6 rectangle have half its perimeter?

Perimeter

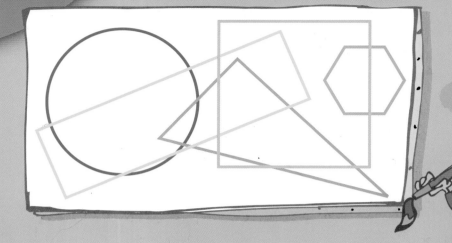

Use a ruler to measure the lengths of the sides of:

1 the square   2 the triangle   3 the rectangle

Write the perimeter of each.

Write the perimeter of:

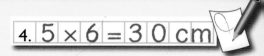
4. 5 × 6 = 3 0 cm

4 a regular pentagon with side length 6 cm

5 a square with side length 4·5 cm

6 a regular hexagon with side length 12 cm

7 a regular octagon with side length 9 cm

8 an equilateral triangle with side length 6·5 cm

9 a regular heptagon with side length 11 cm

If a regular polygon has a perimeter of 72 cm, investigate the possible length of its sides.

Perimeter

What is my perimeter?

1   I am a square.
My area is 25 cm².

2   I am a rectangle. My length is twice my width. My area is 8 cm².

3   I am a regular pentagon. One of my sides is 6 cm long.

What is my area?

4   I am a square.
My perimeter is 24 cm.

5   I am a rectangle. My perimeter is 16 cm. My length is three times my width.

6   I am a square. The number of square centimetres inside me is the same as the number of centimetres around my sides.

For these pin-board shapes, write (a) the perimeter and (b) the area.

7

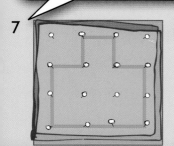

8

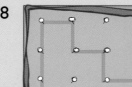

9

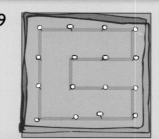

10

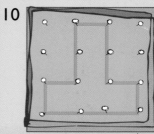

Draw some of your own pin-board shapes, using horizontal and vertical lines only, then find their areas and perimeters.

 **Explore**

5 cm

1 cm

If the sides of rectangles have whole number lengths in centimetres, explore how many different rectangles have a perimeter of 12 cm.

Try rectangles with a perimeter of 14 cm, 16 cm…
Write about any patterns you notice.

Bar graphs

Survey of transport used by 75 people on Thursday

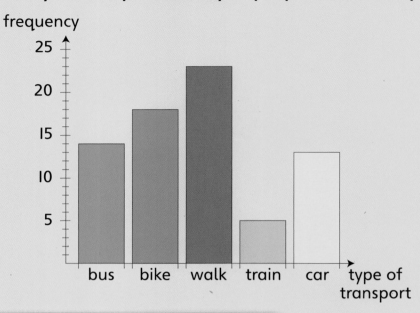

Use the graph to answer these questions.

How many people used a:

1 bus   2 train   3 car

Which method was used by:

4 23 people   5 18 people

How many people used a:

6 bus or train   7 bike or car

8 How many people did not walk?

9 What else can you find out from the graph?

10 Draw a bar graph which you think will show the transport used by children in your class. Is it different in any way?

Bar graphs

Weight of rubbish found

Bin A in shopping mall

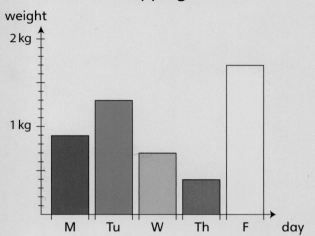

Bin B in bus station

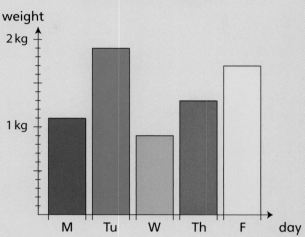

How much rubbish was found:

In Bin A on: 1   Wednesday   2   Friday   3   Monday

In Bin B on: 4   Tuesday   5   Thursday   6   Friday

7   On which days was more rubbish found in the bus station than in the mall?

8   How much less rubbish was found in Bin A than in Bin B on:
   a) Monday   b) Thursday

9   What was the total rubbish found in both bins on:
   a) Thursday   b) Tuesday

10 What was the total rubbish for the 5 days in:
   a) Bin A   b) Bin B

11 Estimate the amount of rubbish in each place on Saturday and Sunday. Explain your estimates.

What could be the reasons why there is a greater weight of rubbish on Tuesdays and Fridays?

47

Bar graphs

Children visiting the museum last week

Mon	Tues	Wed	Thur	Fri	Sat	Sun
24	28	4I	I7	35	53	6I

Draw a bar graph for this frequency table. Have one small square standing for 4 people.

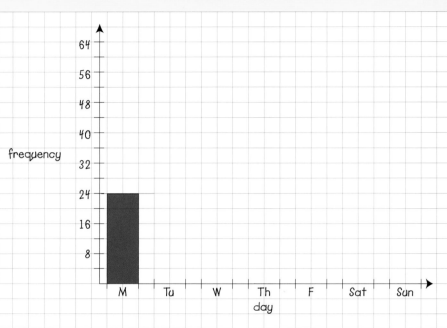

Museum visitors

Use your graph to answer these questions.

1 What was the most popular day?
2 What was the least popular day?

How many more children visited on:
3 Wednesday than Monday   4 Saturday than Wednesday
5 Sunday than Thursday   6 Monday than Thursday

How many people visited:
7 on weekdays   8 at the weekend

9 Explain why you think some days were more popular than others.

Adding

Each child gets some more pocket money. How much do they have now?

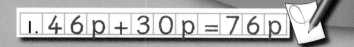

1. 46p + 30p = 76p

1

46p

2

26p

3

23p

4

75p

5

31p

6

42p

7

13p

8

64p

9 Copy and complete the grid.

10	20	30	40	50	60	70	80	90	100
110	120	130			160			190	200
210		230		250		270			300
310	320				360			390	
410		430		450			480		

Write pairs of multiples of 10 that can be added to make 200, for example 110 + 90 = 200.

Adding

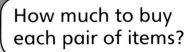
How much to buy each pair of items?

1.
$$70p + 30p = £1·00$$
$$5p + 6p = 11p$$
$$£1·00 + 11p = £1·11$$

1
35p   76p

2
25p   47p

3
17p   65p

4
45p   78p

5
75p   58p

6
56p   74p

7
84p   75p

8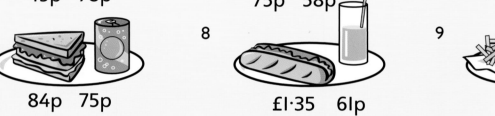
£1·35   61p

9
34p   £1·20

Add 78p to each money box.

10  45p

11  88p

12  60p

13  68p

Add 66p to each purse.

14  85p

15  59p

16  £1·68

17  £1·75

A pizza and a drink come to £1·71. They each cost less than £1. What could the prices be?

Adding

> Add the tens. Add the units. Write the total.

```
1.  40 + 30 + 20 = 90
     5 +  6 +  4 = 15
    90 + 15 = 1 0 5
```

1. 45 + 36 + 24

2. 56 + 48 + 44

3. 27 + 75 + 38

4. 64 + 57 + 35

5. 63 + 77 + 42

6. 74 + 36 + 29

7. 59 + 26 + 44

8. 69 + 77 + 22

9. 57 + 49 + 29

> Choose three balloons. Guess the total, then add the prices.

> Do this six times.

10

75p   48p   66p   59p   84p

> Write three possible 2-digit amounts to complete this addition:
> ☐ p + ☐ p + ☐ p = 50p. Find other possibilities.

Adding

1. $38 + 56 + 46 = 140$ minutes

Choose three programmes. Find the total time. Repeat four times.

1

38 minutes

56 minutes

46 minutes

35 minutes

57 minutes

44 minutes

36 minutes

75 minutes

Choose four programmes. Find the total time. Repeat three times.

Work out the total time spent watching all the programmes. Convert it into hours and minutes.

Add the ticket prices.

2.
$£1 + £1 + £1 = £3$
$40p + 30p + 50p = £1·20$
$6p + 2p + 4p = 12p$
Total $= £4·32$

2
£1·46 £1·32 £1·54

3
£1·55 £1·68 £1·74

4
£1·36 £1·65 £1·88

5
£1·27 £1·33 £1·64

6
£1·37 £1·72 £1·24

7
£1·57 £1·42 £1·33

Subtracting

Subtraction **D2**

Write how much to reach each target.

$$36 \overset{}{\underset{4}{\frown}} 40 \overset{}{\underset{20}{\frown}} 60 = 24$$

1. $36 + 24 = 60$

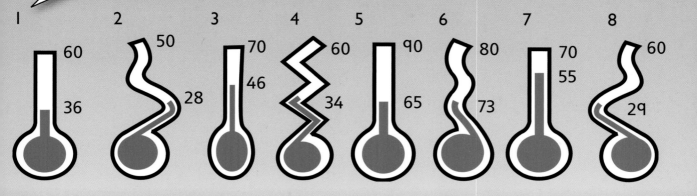

| 1 | 2 | 3 | 4 | 5 | 6 | 7 | 8 |

1. 60 / 36
2. 50 / 28
3. 70 / 46
4. 60 / 34
5. 90 / 65
6. 80 / 73
7. 70 / 55
8. 60 / 29

Write the difference in the numbers of fish eaten by each cat.

9. $61 - 37 = 24$

9. 61 fish 37 fish

10. 73 fish 28 fish

11. 86 fish 52 fish

12. 58 fish 23 fish

13. 77 fish 38 fish

14. 68 fish 49 fish

15. 74 fish 36 fish

16. 56 fish 39 fish

Two numbers have a difference of 35. They are both between 50 and 100. What could the numbers be?

53

Subtracting

Write how many more fish the big shark eats.

54　60　83
　6　　23　= 29

1. $83 - 54 = 29$ fish

1

83 fish　54 fish

2

72 fish　38 fish

3

68 fish　24 fish

4

94 fish　52 fish

5

76 fish　48 fish

6

85 fish　67 fish

7

56 fish　37 fish

8

77 fish　59 fish

Copy and complete.

9. $306 - 287 = 19$

9

$306 - 287 =$

10

$204 - 176 =$

11
$110 - 87 =$

12

$301 - 275 =$

13

$408 - 378 =$

14
$207 - 188 =$

15
$302 - 284 =$

16
$111 - 96 =$

17
$314 - 297 =$

How many pairs of numbers between 45 and 65 have a difference of 5?

Subtracting

Write how much each diver has left.

1. $46p - 6p = 40p$

1 46p – 6p

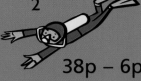

2 38p – 6p

3 54p – 3p

4 61p – 1p

5 75p – 3p

6 34p – 2p

7 45p – 4p

8 63p – 3p

9 76p – 5p

What if each diver had only 10p left? What would each one have lost?

With a partner, explore what happens when you take away one more than the units digit from a 2-digit number, for example $46 - 7 = \boxed{}$.

Copy and complete.

10. $84 - 16 = 68$

10 84 – 16 =

11 72 – 28 =

12 63 – 27 =

13 55 – 18 =

14 73 – 36 =

15 64 – 19 =

16 58 – 29 =

17 61 – 15 =

18 74 – 26 =

Subtracting

How tall is each bush after being cut?

1. 8 2 – 1 8 = 6 4 cm

1

82 cm 18 cm cut

2

73 cm 36 cm cut

3

94 cm 25 cm cut

4

65 cm 28 cm cut

5

71 cm 27 cm cut

6

63 cm 15 cm cut

7

208 cm 32 cm cut

8

183 cm 58 cm cut

9

274 cm 37 cm cut

Draw your own bush and write its height.
Write a subtraction to cut it in half. Keep going.

Find the difference between each pair of cards.

10   11   12   13   14   15

| 183 | 47 | | 188 | 221 | | 144 | 86 | | 164 | 55 | | 187 | 214 | | 136 | 372 |

Choose the largest and the smallest number.
Find the difference between them.

Adding and subtracting

Write each new price.

```
1. 75p − 20p = 55p
   55p + 1p = 56p
```

1

75p
19p off

2

68p
29p off

3

57p
19p off

4

63p
29p off

5

78p
19p off

6

54p
29p off

Write the amount to buy both comics.

```
7. 46p + 30p = 76p
   76p − 1p = 75p
```

7

GOAL! 46p
DJ 29p

8

GLAM 56p
Super Heroes 9p

9

DINO WEEKLY 74p
GIRL 19p

10

SPLAT 28p
ROCK 59p

11

Astro Girl 45p
Toons 39p

12

DANCE 63p
RUGBY 29p

Work with a partner. They choose a 2-digit number.
You subtract 9. They subtract 9 from your answer.
Keep going like this. How many times do you subtract 9?

Adding and subtracting

How many bricks now?

1. 138 + 39 = 177 bricks ✓

1

138 bricks, 39 more

2

125 bricks, 49 more

3

243 bricks, 29 more

4

176 bricks, 19 more

5

136 bricks, 69 more

6

217 bricks, 39 more

Copy and complete.

7   87 − 29 =

8   133 − 41 =

9   256 − 19 =

10 84 − 39 =

11 300 − 49 =

12 110 − 31 =

Write some subtractions like this one: 35 − 29, where the tens digit in the first number is only 1 more than the tens digit in the second number. Do the subtractions. What do you notice?

13 A film lasts 126 minutes. Jane and her dad left after 79 minutes. How much did they miss?

14 Asif has earned £193. His grandma gives him a bonus of £59. How much does he have now?

15 Chang rode 72 miles on her bike. For the last 29 miles her gears were not working. For how many miles were the gears working?

16 Tom runs 126 m from his house to the park, then runs 59 m round the park. How far does he run in total?
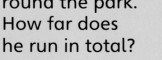

Adding and subtracting

Find the difference between the number of miles travelled by each car.

1. $246 - 59 = 187$ miles

Use the nearest multiple of 10. You can choose whether to count back or count on.

1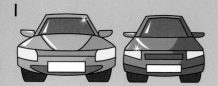

246 miles   59 miles

2

427 miles   79 miles

3

154 miles   88 miles

4

285 miles   79 miles

5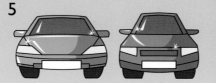

274 miles   57 miles

6

164 miles   89 miles

7

How many centimetres must each snail crawl to reach the lettuce?

7. (a) $247 - 39 = 208$ cm

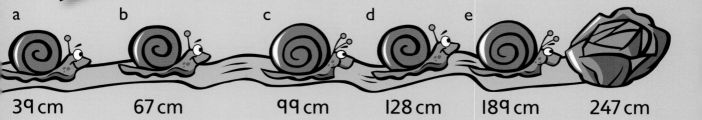

a   b   c   d   e

39 cm   67 cm   99 cm   128 cm   189 cm   247 cm

Work with a partner. Agree who will count back and who will count on. Try this subtraction: 167 – 89. Reverse roles. Which is the best method for you? Try 224 – 129.

Adding and subtracting

Write the new prices.

1. £179 + £29 = £208

1
£179
£29 price rise

2
£245
£58 off

3
£157
£39 price rise

4
£161
£39 off

5
£222
£59 off

6
£260
£37 price rise

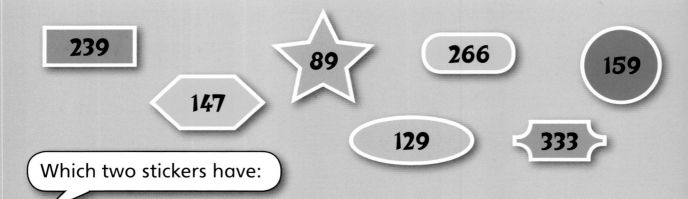

239

89

266

159

147

129

333

Which two stickers have:

7 a total of 236

8 a difference of 107

9 the greatest total (599)

10 the smallest total (218)

11 the greatest difference (244)

12 the smallest difference (12)

Write your own questions about totals or differences of pairs of these stickers.

Adding

Add the two numbers.

1. $40 + 30 + 7 + 8 =$
   $70 + 15 = 85$

| 1 | 47 + 38 | 2 | 54 + 47 | 3 | 62 + 74 |

| 4 | 36 + 68 | 5 | 75 + 87 | 6 | 53 + 71 |

Use the method shown here to complete the additions below.

7.
```
 (7 0 0)
 H T U
 5 6 3
+  8 8
 ─────
     1 1
   1 4 0
   5 0 0
 ─────
   6 5 1
```
add units (3 + 8)
add tens (60 + 80)
add hundreds (500)
grand total

```
7     5 6 3
    +   8 8
    ───────
    ───────
```

```
8     6 4 2
    +   7 6
    ───────
    ───────
```

```
9     5 8 4
    + 1 7 7
    ───────
    ───────
```

```
10    6 8 4
    + 2 7 7
    ───────
    ───────
```

```
11    4 7 9
    + 3 5 4
    ───────
    ───────
```

```
12    6 4 8
    + 2 5 6
    ───────
    ───────
```

Use one of each of these digits: 2 7 5 4 6

to create an addition like this: ☐ ☐ ☐
                              +   ☐ ☐

to get the answer 636. Can you do the same for 609 and 312?

Adding

How many grams of gold does each pair of gold diggers have in total?

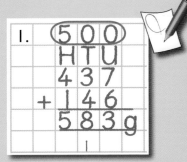

1.
	5	0	0
	H	T	U
	4	3	7
+	1	4	6
	5	8	3	g

1

146 g   437 g

2

378 g   166 g

3

526 g   219 g

4

176 g   359 g

5

468 g   129 g

6

336 g   158 g

7

Choose two water pouches. Write an approximate total.

Work out the addition. Repeat six times.

 342 ml
 686 ml
 455 ml
 548 ml
 189 ml

Work with a partner to find ways of using the digits
1 2 3 4 5 6 7   to make this addition work:

☐☐☐ + ☐☐☐ = ☐ 0 0

Adding

Each child does three jumps. Find the total length.

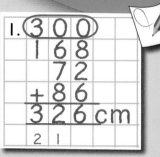

```
1. 300
   168
    72
  + 86
  326 cm
   2 1
```

1

168 cm
72 cm
86 cm

2

154 cm
65 cm
23 cm

3

176 cm
54 cm
39 cm

4

165 cm
38 cm
46 cm

5

159 cm
78 cm
24 cm

Work with a partner. Use the digits 1 2 3 4 5 6 7
to get the largest possible total from this addition:

☐☐ + ☐☐ + ☐☐ =

6   Omar drives 285 miles to London
and a further 126 miles to Bristol.
He then drives 168 miles to Cornwall.
How far does he drive in total?

7   Emma's puppy is 1 year and 85 days old
today. How many days has she lived?
If she was born on 1st January,
what is today's date?

8   Annie has weighed her ingredients. She has
864 g of flour and 275 g of sugar. She adds
189 g of butter. What is the total weight?

Adding

Choose three videos. Guess the total running time.
Add the numbers and work it out. Repeat six times.

1

126 minutes

98 minutes

87 minutes

119 minutes

145 minutes

137 minutes

Explore

£368   £467   £459   £386   £555

Choose three cheques to make the largest total possible.

Write your guess first, then do the addition.

Now choose the three cheques that give the second largest total.

Continue like this.

Write the ten different cheque totals in order, largest to smallest.

Sixes

Write how many eggs.

1. $3 \times 6 = 18$

1

2

3

4

5

6

7

8

9

Which number of eggs between 40 and 50 will fit exactly in boxes of 6?

Write how many boxes can be filled with these eggs:

10. $18 \div 6 = 3$ boxes

10
18 eggs

11
30 eggs

12
54 eggs

13
36 eggs

14
24 eggs

15
42 eggs

65

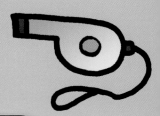

1 Complete the 3s, then double to complete the 6s.

3s	3	6	9	12						
6s	6									

2 Complete the 1s and 5s, then add to complete the 6s.

1s	1	2	3	4							
5s	5	10									
6s	6										

3 Find the 6s by adding the 2s and 4s.

 Find the 12s by doubling the 6s.
Write some ×12 facts, for example 7 × 12 = ☐

Copy and complete.

4  4 × 3 = ... → 4 × 6 = ...

5 7 × 3 = ... → 7 × 6 = ...

6 9 × 3 = ... → 9 × 6 = ...

7 11 × 3 = ... → 11 × 6 = ...

8 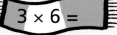 3 × 6 =   **9** 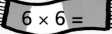 8 × 6 =   **10** 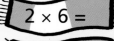 2 × 6 =

11 5 × 6 =   **12** 6 × 6 =   **13** 20 × 6 =

Sixes

Write the position of the pointer on each counting stick.

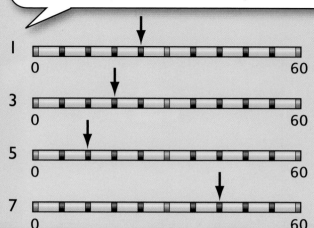

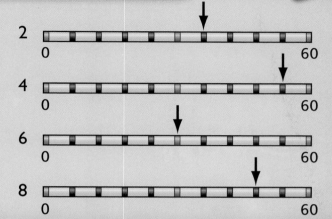

9   47 oranges are put into bags of six. How many bags are there and how many oranges are left over?

10 Stickers are 6p each. Sanjay has a £1 coin, and he buys one sticker every day for a week. How much has he left?

11 Katie works in the corner shop on every day except Sunday. How many days will Katie have worked after 9 weeks?

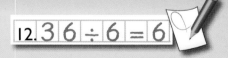

Write your own word problem for this division: $24 \div 6 = 4$.

Copy and complete.

12. $36 \div 6 = 6$

12 $36 \div 6 = \square$ 13 $18 \div 6 = \square$ 14 $42 \div 6 = \square$

15 $12 \div 6 = \square$ 16 $54 \div 6 = \square$ 17 $60 \div 6 = \square$

18 $24 \div 6 = \square$ 19 $30 \div 6 = \square$ 20 $48 \div 6 = \square$

21 one-sixth of 42 is $\square$ 22 five-sixths of 24 is $\square$

Copy and write the missing numbers.

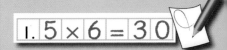
1. 5 × 6 = 30

1   5 × 6 =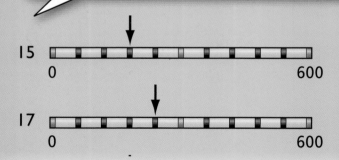

2   7 × 6 =

3   18 ÷ 6 =

4   36 ÷ 6 =

5   × 6 = 12

6   × 6 = 54

7   ÷ 6 = 10

8   ÷ 6 = 4

9   3 × = 18

10 8 × 6 =

11 ÷ 6 = 1

12 ÷ 6 = 9

13 48 ÷ 6 =

14 × 6 = 24

Write the position of the pointer on each stick.

15
0   600

16
0   600

17
0   600

18
0   600

Copy and complete.

19 7 × 60 =

20 2 × 60 =

21 9 × 60 =

22 3 × 60 =

23 120 ÷ 60 =

24 360 ÷ 60 =

25 4 × 60 =

26 480 ÷ 60 =

27 300 ÷ 60 =

Eights

Each boat in the race has eight rowers. Write the number of rowers.

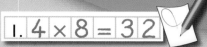 1. 4 × 8 = 32

1

2

3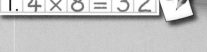

4 6 boats   5 8 boats   6 7 boats

Write how many boats are needed for these rowers:

7

16 rowers

8

48 rowers

9

56 rowers

10 24 rowers   11 32 rowers   12 80 rowers

If each boat can only take six rowers, how many boats are needed each time? Are there any spaces left?

69

Eights

Write the position of each pointer on the counting sticks.

1
0   80

2
0   80

3
0   80

4
0   80

5
0   80

6
0   80

The children hold up one finger for each 8. Write how many they have counted.

7. $4 \times 8 = 32$

7

8

9

10

11

12

How many fingers show multiples of 10?
How many hands are needed to show 240?

Copy and complete.

13. $2 \times 8 = 16$

13   $2 \times 8 = \boxed{}$

14   $7 \times 8 = \boxed{}$

15   $5 \times 8 = \boxed{}$

16   $32 \div 8 = \boxed{}$

17   $11 \times 8 = \boxed{}$

18   $64 \div 8 = \boxed{}$

19   $6 \times 8 = \boxed{}$

20   $9 \times 8 = \boxed{}$

21   $0 \times 8 = \boxed{}$

22   $24 \div 8 = \boxed{}$

23   $8 \div 8 = \boxed{}$

24   $20 \times 8 = \boxed{}$

Eights

1 Complete the 4s, then double to complete the 8s.

4s	4	8	12	16							
8s	8										

2 Complete the 3s and 5s, then add to complete the 8s.

3s	3	6	9								
5s	5	10									
8s	8										

3 Find a way of using the 6s to help find the 8s.

 Write the ×16 multiplication table. Could you write the ×32 table?

Copy and complete.

4 $5 \times 8 =$

5 $4 \times 8 =$

6 $9 \times 8 =$

7 $7 \times 8 =$

8 $2 \times 8 =$

9 $12 \times 8 =$

10 A badge costs 8p. How many badges can Tom buy with two 20p coins, one 5p coin, one 2p coin and one 1p coin?

11 At the fair you can have three balls at the coconut shy for 8p. How many balls can you have with a 50p coin?

Copy and write the missing numbers.

1. $3 \times 8 = 24$

1   $3 \times 8 =$

2   $5 \times 8 =$

3   $16 \div 8 =$

4   $80 \div 8 =$

5   $\times 8 = 56$

6   $\times 8 = 32$

7   $\div 8 = 6$

8   $\div 8 = 3$

9   $9 \times 8 =$

10   $\times 8 = 64$

11   $\div 8 = 4$

12   $\div 8 = 1$

13   $10 \times 8 =$

14   $20 \times 8 =$

15   $24 \div 8 =$

 **Explore**

These are the multiples of 4:   4   8   12   16   20
These are their units digits: 4   8   2   6   0

Use them to write the units digits of the multiples of 8:   8   6   ...

Use these to write the units digits of the multiples of 16.

What do you notice?

Copy and complete.

16   $3 \times 80 =$

17   $6 \times 80 =$

18   $5 \times 80 =$

19   $4 \times 80 =$

20   $7 \times 80 =$

21   $9 \times 80 =$

22   $160 \div 80 =$

23   $400 \div 80 =$

24   $640 \div 80 =$

Ordering fractions

Write each pair of fractions, smallest first.

1

2

3

4

5
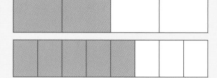

6

7
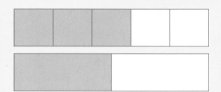

8

Write the three fractions in order, smallest first.

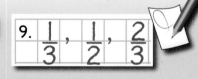

9
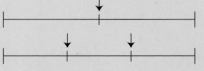

10

11
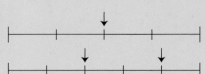

12

Use the last pair of number lines to write five fractions in order.

73

Ordering fractions

Write the pairs of pizzas as fractions, using <.

1. $\dfrac{1}{3} < \dfrac{1}{2}$

1

2

3

4

5

6

Look at the fractions you have written. Write them in order, smallest first.

Write <, > or = between each pair.

7. $\dfrac{1}{2} < \dfrac{2}{3}$

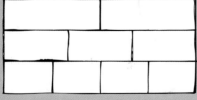

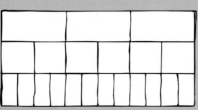

7 $\dfrac{1}{2}$ $\dfrac{2}{3}$ 8 $\dfrac{1}{3}$ $\dfrac{1}{4}$ 9 $\dfrac{2}{3}$ $\dfrac{3}{4}$ 10 $\dfrac{2}{4}$ $\dfrac{1}{2}$

11 $\dfrac{1}{4}$ $\dfrac{1}{2}$ 12 $\dfrac{2}{3}$ $\dfrac{2}{4}$ 13 $\dfrac{1}{3}$ $\dfrac{5}{12}$ 14 $\dfrac{7}{12}$ $\dfrac{2}{3}$

15 $\dfrac{5}{6}$ $\dfrac{2}{3}$ 16 $\dfrac{1}{6}$ $\dfrac{1}{3}$ 17 $\dfrac{3}{6}$ $\dfrac{6}{12}$ 18 $\dfrac{5}{6}$ $\dfrac{11}{12}$

19 $\dfrac{2}{3}$ $\dfrac{8}{12}$ 20 $\dfrac{3}{12}$ $\dfrac{1}{6}$ 21 $\dfrac{4}{6}$ $\dfrac{2}{3}$

Ordering fractions

Use the lines to help you write each set of fractions in order, smallest to largest.

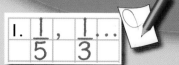

1. $\frac{1}{5}$, $\frac{1}{3}$ ...

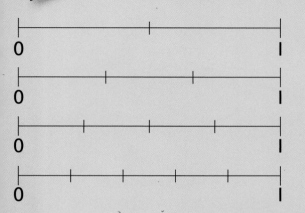

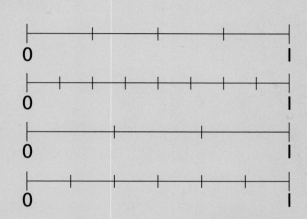

1   $\frac{1}{3}$, $\frac{2}{4}$, $\frac{1}{5}$, $\frac{2}{3}$, $\frac{3}{5}$

2   $\frac{4}{5}$, $\frac{1}{3}$, $\frac{1}{4}$, $\frac{2}{5}$, $\frac{2}{4}$

3   $\frac{3}{6}$, $\frac{2}{8}$, $\frac{1}{3}$, $\frac{3}{4}$, $\frac{7}{8}$

4   $\frac{4}{5}$, $\frac{3}{4}$, $\frac{1}{2}$, $\frac{1}{4}$, $\frac{2}{5}$

5   $\frac{3}{4}$, $\frac{2}{3}$, $\frac{5}{6}$, $\frac{3}{8}$, $\frac{1}{6}$

6   $\frac{5}{8}$, $\frac{2}{3}$, $\frac{1}{8}$, $\frac{2}{4}$, $\frac{3}{8}$

7   $\frac{3}{4}$, $\frac{2}{3}$, $\frac{3}{5}$, $\frac{1}{2}$, $\frac{2}{5}$

8   $\frac{1}{8}$, $\frac{5}{8}$, $\frac{2}{3}$, $\frac{1}{3}$, $\frac{2}{4}$

9   $\frac{1}{6}$, $\frac{3}{4}$, $\frac{7}{8}$, $\frac{1}{3}$, $\frac{4}{5}$

 Write some fractions between $\frac{1}{2}$ and $\frac{3}{4}$.

Explore

Use these cards: 1   2   3   4   5   6

Make pairs of fractions, one smaller than the other: $\frac{1}{6}$ < $\frac{2}{5}$

How many pairs can you make?
How many equal pairs can you make?

Ordering fractions

I am a fraction. Guess who I am.

1 My bottom number is 4. I am less than $\frac{1}{3}$.

2 My top number is 3. I am more than $\frac{2}{3}$.

3 My top and bottom numbers have a total of 9. I am the same size as $\frac{1}{2}$.

4 My bottom number is double my top number and they have a total of 12.

5 My top number is 2 less than my bottom number. I am the same size as $\frac{3}{4}$.

6 I am more than $\frac{1}{4}$ and less than $\frac{1}{2}$.

 Invent your own 'Guess who I am' fractions.

Write the missing numbers.

Some may have more than one answer.

 7. 1, 2

7 $\frac{\square}{5} < \frac{1}{2}$

8 $\frac{\square}{8} < \frac{3}{4}$

9 $\frac{\square}{3} < \frac{1}{2}$

10 $\frac{\square}{4} < \frac{5}{8}$

11 $\frac{1}{2} < \frac{\square}{6}$

12 $\frac{2}{3} = \frac{\square}{12}$

13 $\frac{\square}{8} > \frac{1}{2}$

14 $\frac{3}{5} > \frac{\square}{4}$

15 $\frac{\square}{8} < \frac{1}{4}$

16 $\frac{5}{6} > \frac{\square}{3}$

17 $\frac{4}{16} = \frac{\square}{4}$

18 $\frac{4}{6} = \frac{\square}{3}$

Tenths

Write each as a fraction.

1. $\frac{3}{10}$

1

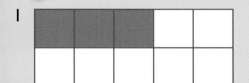

2

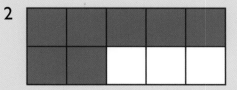

3

4

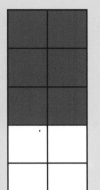

5

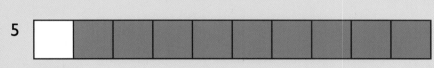

6

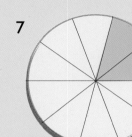

7

Write each as a decimal.

1. $0\cdot3$

Write these in order, smallest to largest.

8. $0\cdot6, \frac{7}{10}, $ eight-tenths

8 $0\cdot6$, eight-tenths, $\frac{7}{10}$

9   four-tenths, $0\cdot3$, $\frac{5}{10}$

10   seven-tenths, $0\cdot9$, $\frac{8}{10}$

11 $0\cdot7$, $\frac{3}{10}$, $0\cdot5$

12 $\frac{5}{10}$, $\frac{8}{10}$, $0\cdot6$

13 $\frac{3}{10}$, $\frac{1}{2}$, $0\cdot4$

Write your own sets of fractions and decimals.
Swap with your partner and put them in order.

Write each as a mixed number.

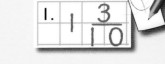
1. $1\frac{3}{10}$

1

2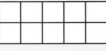

3

4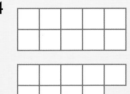

5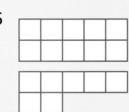

6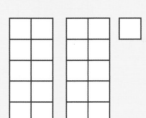

Write each as a decimal.

1. $1·3$

Write how many tenths in each number.

7. $1\frac{3}{10}$

7 $1\frac{3}{10}$

8 $2\frac{1}{10}$

9 $3\frac{6}{10}$

10 $4\frac{4}{10}$

11 $11\frac{7}{10}$

12 $3\frac{1}{2}$

13 $1\frac{1}{5}$

14 $2·3$

15 $1·7$

16 $7\frac{1}{2}$

17 $0·6$

18 $4·3$

Write the fractions in order, smallest to largest.
Choose two of them that are next-door numbers.
Ask your partner to write a number in between.

Tenths

Write the position of these pointers.

1. (a) 1·8

d   g   c   a   h   e   b   f

0   1   2   3   4

Collect 10 tokens for a free tub of ice-cream. Write how many tubs you can have with these tokens.

2. 2·3 tubs

| 2 | 23 tokens | 3 | 47 tokens | 4 | 16 tokens |
| 5 | 38 tokens | 6 | 54 tokens | 7 | 79 tokens |

How many more tokens would you need to get a complete number of tubs each time?

🔍 Explore

Use one of each of these cards: 3   7   2   5

Make different decimal numbers like this:

How many can you make between 3·3 and 7·3?

How many can you make that are not between these numbers?

Write them in order, smallest first.

Write the weight of each animal.

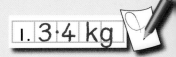

1

2

3

4

5

6

Write each weight in grams.

What animals do you think would be 10 times heavier than these?

Write the decimal number that is half-way between each pair.

7   1·5   2·5

8   1·2   1·8

9   3·3   3·9

10   2 $\frac{3}{10}$ 3·3

11   1·8   2·4

12   1 $\frac{7}{10}$ 3·7

13   1·4   3·6

14   2·6   5·8